CARING FOR YOUR RAT

How to care for your Rat and everything you need to know to keep them well

WRITTEN BY VETERINARY EXPERT

DR. GORDON ROBERTS BVSC MRCVS

Hello! My name is Gordon Roberts and I'm the author of this book. I hope you enjoy all of the specialist advice it contains. I'm a huge advocate of preventative care for animals, and I'd love to see more pet owners taking the time to research their pet's health care needs.

Being proactive and educating yourself about your pet's health now, rather than later on, could save you and your pet a lot of trouble in the long run.

If you'd like to read more of my professional pet care advice simply go to my website at http://drgordonroberts.com/freereportsdownload/.

As a thank you for purchasing this book, you'll find dozens of bonus pet care reports there to download and keep, absolutely free of charge!

Best wishes,

Gordon
Founder, Wellpets

Contents

~

Introduction

Are you ready to welcome one of the most charismatic, intelligent creatures of the pet world into your home? This book will tell you all you need to know (and more) about the wonderful rat. Whether you are just starting out as a rat owner or you'd like to know more about looking after a rat you already have, the following chapters will guide you through the journey of becoming a conscientious, knowledgeable pet owner. You will learn how to make your rat as happy as he makes you, with some easy tips and useful information on every aspect of rat care. There are two ways to use this book: you can either read it from start to finish, to make sure you don't miss anything vital or, if you prefer, you can skip to the chapters that interest you most. Either way, this handy guide can be kept to refer back to again and again throughout your rat's life. So, hold on tight – it's going to be a fun ride! We hope you enjoy it.

Chapter 1:
Learning about the rat

Rats aren't the first furry creature that springs to mind when you think of a house pet, but those that have kept them know that they're one of the best kept secrets in the pet world. More intelligent than hamsters, gerbils, rabbits and guinea pigs put together, with bags of personality, they are an animal which grows on you and becomes both a friend and a family member. If you're just starting out as a rat owner, this chapter will tell you some fascinating and useful facts about the humble rat.

Why keep rats as pets?

Rats are cheeky, amusing, clever and big enough to ride around on your shoulder or sit in your lap without scurrying away like a hamster or a gerbil might. They are a lot more responsive to human companionship than, for example, guinea pigs, and a lot less timid. They are, without a doubt, the thinking man's pet.

Rats around the world

In the West, rats don't have such a great reputation – just mention to someone that you're planning to keep a rat as a pet and you'll get a range of shocked responses. This is because many people in Europe and the U.S. still don't know that rats can be amazing pets. In other parts of the world, however, it's a very different story.

Here are some fascinating ways the rat is viewed around the world:

- In China, the rat is a sign of prosperity and is the first animal sign in the zodiac, due to its revered intelligence
- Japan also considers the rat to be a sign of wealth and there is a Japanese legend in which one of the seven lucky gods, Daikoku (god of wealth and good fortune), is helped by a rat
- In India, the rat is also celebrated as being godly: the Hindu god Ganesha rides on the back of rats
- Both Ancient Rome and Ancient Egypt worshipped the rat as a symbol of good luck

So, there you have it. Some of the world's eastern countries have recognised the rat's spiritual essence and made it a part of their culture. Tell that to the next person who is shocked that you have a pet rat!

Myths about rats

To give you even more of a well-rounded picture of rats, we're now going to debunk some of the common myths around these animals. If you're going to become a rat enthusiast, it's important to address these issues so that you can be the best possible ambassador for these fantastic pets.

Myth: Rats carry diseases and were responsible for the plague.
Truth: Recent research has shown that it was probably the rat flea,

and not the rat, which caused the plague back in the 1300s. And even then, it is more accurate to say that the flea which these animals carried was the animal that was truly responsible.

When it comes to diseases, it is highly unlikely for today's domesticated rat to carry any form of disease that could be passed on to humans they are always bred in captivity and have been given the same standard of veterinary care as any other pet.

Myth: Rats bite a lot
Truth: Rats are actually calmer and more docile than hamsters, gerbils and mice and they are larger, so they rarely feel threatened enough to bite you. They seldom bite and usually just want to satisfy their curiosity about you and make friends (especially if you have a tasty treat to feed them!).

Myth: Rats have teeth that constantly grow
Truth: Unlike hamsters and other rodents, the rat has teeth that he can grind down easily by rubbing the top and bottom teeth together. They do grow constantly, but it is highly unlikely that your rat's teeth will become overgrown enough to pose a problem.

Rat history

The first rats were domesticated (kept in captivity) in the 1800s. In Britain, a sport called "ratting" became very popular at that time which led to a lot of people keeping their own rats in cages. Ratting was a cruel sport which involved dogs (usually terriers) being put into pits with rats, where they were pitted against other dogs to see who could kill the most rats.

Rats, sadly, became valuable currency and at first thousands of them were captured from the wild and sold off. Later on, they were bred in captivity and this led to them eventually being kept as family pets.

In the early 1900s, rats became briefly fashionable and an English group called the National Mouse Club changed their name to the National Mouse and Rat Club and began showing rats at pet shows.

Unfortunately, rats fell out of favour and they went back to showing only mice. The rat had a long time to wait before it eventually became popular again in 1976, when the National Fancy Rat Society was set up. From then on, rats were kept mostly as children's pets.

They were the focus of some fantastic children's stories and films, including Beatrix Potter stories, the fairytale Cinderella and the amazing book The Rats of Nimh. Give these books to your children if they are rat enthusiasts! In the 1990s rats finally went mainstream, and they became well known pets kept by both children and adults alike in the UK and in the U.S. especially.

The rat family

Rats belong to the rodent family, and they are thought to be among the most intelligent of this huge and diverse species, along with the squirrel. The word "rodent" comes from the latin word rodere which means "to gnaw". All rodents have one thing in common: a set of front teeth (known as incisors) on the top and bottom jaws, which grow throughout the animal's life.

Rodents make up about 40% of all mammals on earth, making them one of nature's most successful creatures. They are one of the most diverse species, with some living in trees, some being semi-aquatic and some even thriving in human habitats. With these impressive biological credentials, the rat is not just a common house pet – he is a creature with wild and fascinating origins.

Rat species

There are many wild species of rat around the world, with different habitats and appearances. They include the wood rat, the mole rat, the kangaroo rat and the cotton rat. Some rats look typically rat-like and others look very different to the rats we usually think of, being only distant relatives to their other rat cousins. This makes rats pretty fascinating as a species, because they are so diverse.

Most pet rats today are the Norway rat species, or Rattus norvegicus. Only very rarely will you find another type of domesticated rat, Rattus rattus (or the black rat) in captivity, which is thought to have originated from India where it jumped on board the ships of explorers and travelled the world. The Norway rat, contrary to its name, actually came from Russia and was mistakenly named the Norway rat by the British who assumed it had hopped on board ships in Norway and travelled throughout Europe that way. In general, the Norway rat is heavier and larger than it's black rat cousins and is suited to cool climates.

We've talked a bit about where the rat comes from and how he came to be kept as a pet. Now it's time to go a little bit deeper and explore the rat's biology and behaviour. The more you know about your rat, the better you will be at keeping him healthy and happy. So, let's begin.

The life cycle of a rat

Rats are born in litters of between eight and twelve pups and they are completely blind and furless for the first few days of their lives. After about two weeks, their eyes will open and they will start to eat solid foods rather than their mother's milk. Once they are about 5 weeks old, they are old enough to have their own babies – amazingly! Once a female falls pregnant she will carry her pups for about twenty-one to twenty-three days, after which time they will be born, and the next generation of rat pups begin their lives.

How long do rats live for?
Rats in captivity live for between two and three years, though many well cared for rats have surprised their owners by living longer than this, due to a combination of good genetics and excellent care from their owners.

How big do rats grow?
Those that have only kept gerbils or hamsters in the past may take a while to get used to the rat's larger size. This is a blessing in disguise as it makes them cuddlier and easier to handle than other rodent pets. On average rats grow between six and ten inches long, not including their tails. Usually male rats are slightly larger and can weigh up to two pounds.

The sleep cycle of rats

Rats are nocturnal, meaning that they are at their most active at night time. There are a few things to bear in mind with any nocturnal pet. The first is that you need to place their cage somewhere that is peaceful in the day time, so that your little friends can get their beauty sleep. The cage also needs to be away from your bedroom as your rats are going to be running around, chewing and getting up to mischief through the night which can easily wake up a light sleeper. Lastly, nocturnal pets aren't ideal for young children because they will wake up just as the children are going to bed at night.

Rats are social creatures

Rats are social creatures and like to live in pairs or groups, so you should not just get a single rat – your little friend needs a playmate to be happy.

Rat facts

You've heard a little bit about the rat's history and origins, but there is so much more to learn about these fascinating creatures. As a rat owner, you need to find out as much as you can about what life is like for a rat so that you can understand your pet and what makes him happy.

Here are some basic facts you should learn before we go any further:

- Rats have surprisingly poor eyesight, but very strong noses and ears to make up for this. They are colour blind and don't see well in the dark, although their whiskers can help them to detect movement and their noses help them to smell their way around. One good feature that they have though is the ability to see in two directions at once – their eyes are well placed on either side of the head in order to allow them to do this, which means that they can easily spot predators approaching.
- Rats have also adapted to use their urine as a scent marker as they travel, so that they can easily follow their own trail back to where they came from.
- Rats are physically unable to throw up because they have an extremely strong wall between their stomach and their oesophagus.
- Rats can detect a microscopic amount of poison in their food from a considerable distance, which is one reason that they have survived decades of attempted poisonings from humans
- Rats are very sensitive to electromagnetic fields in their environments, which means that if there are a lot of electrical devices around their cages they will probably be very unhappy.
- Rats don't like to have their bellies stroked, especially by people they don't really know or trust. They also prefer to be stroked in the direction of their fur, like a lot of animals.
- Rats, like a lot of pets, can sense if you're nervous, angry or unhappy. It's best to handle them only when you're in a good mood or they will feel very uneasy.

Rat behaviour in brief

Good pet owners know the complexity of their pets and take the time to understand their behaviours. Here are some behaviours you might notice in your rat. Not all of them are desirable behaviours, but if you are going to own one of these fascinating creatures, you need to take the good with the bad!

Squeaking and other sounds: Rats, unlike hamsters and mice, make a range of noises. They are not silent creatures! At any given time, you can expect your rat to squeak, chirp, hiss and peep. Usually these vocalisations are sounds of alarm, protest or stress. So, when you hear these sounds coming from your rat it's a good way to gauge how they are feeling and reacting to something in their environment. During confrontations with other rats, you'll usually hear these sounds (and if so, you should probably separate the rats). We know from research that a rat can produce a high pitched sound that signifies pleasure, but this sound is beyond a human's range of hearing.

Teeth grinding: Rats do this to actually grind down their teeth down. Sometimes they do it in times of stress, although some rat owners report that they also do it at times when they feel contented, a bit like purring.

Eye bulging: As the rat grinds its teeth, the eyes will naturally bulge from their sockets. It's nothing to be alarmed about.

Whisker twitching: The whiskers are your rat's means of feeling and sensing the objects he encounters. The twitching allows the whiskers to move over an object or a surface that your rat comes across to get sensory information.

Play fighting: In young rats, play fighting, chasing, and pinning each other to the ground is quite common. After one month of age, it usually declines.

Adult fighting: Adult males can sometimes be seen chasing, boxing and rolling each other on their backs whilst squeaking. Rats reach adulthood at 5-6 months old, and at this time they may start to fight to establish dominance. Once a dominant male emerges, the fighting usually calms down because a hierarchy has been established. Fighting can also happen when a new rat is introduced to the colony, which is never a good idea as there is less room to run for cover in a confined space like a cage. It's important to be a responsible owner and not keep rats together if they are fighting a lot – this will only stress them and make for a very unhappy life for the rats.

Scent marking: Rats use their urine to mark their scent on places, people and other rats that they encounter. Both males and females do this. Scent marking serves all sorts of functions, from signalling the presence of rats of the opposite sex, to navigation in places they may be unfamiliar with. So, it is natural, normal behaviour.

Ear wiggling: When a female rat comes into heat (when she is ready to find a mate), she will display an odd behaviour where the ears will wiggle back and forth, sometimes very rapidly.

Tail wagging: In times of tension or excitement, your rat might lash its tail from side to side. It might be the whole tail or just the tip.

Swaying from side to side: It's thought that some rats do this as a way to gauge distances and it might be the result of poor eyesight.

Chapter 3:
Preparing for your rats

Now that you know enough about rats to choose to keep them as pets, it's time to make some preparations for becoming a rat owner. This section will go through all the things you need to have ready before bringing home your new pets.

Before the final decision

When it comes to bringing any new pet into your life, you need to ab-solutely sure that you are making the right decision, and that you can commit to looking after these small animals. So, before you rush out and invest in all the rat equipment mentioned in this chapter, make sure you can answer all of the following questions:

- *Do I have any other commitments which might prevent me from looking after my rats? For example, do I have a new baby arriving, or other pets which might already pose a big enough task to look after?*
- *Am I sure that there will be someone to look after my rats if I go on holiday?*
- *Do I have the money for all the rat food and equipment that I need to invest in?*
- *Do I have a suitable home for the rats, with space away from larger pets and noisy environments?*

Are your children old enough for small pets?

Over the years, the rat has slowly gained a reputation as a children's pet, and they are usually given as a first pet to kids who may be asking for something bigger and more costly such as a puppy. Whilst rats make fantastic first-time pets for children, you need to be aware that they are small, fragile and can easily go missing if they escape or are allowed to roam free.

Children should first be educated on how to handle a rat and what is acceptable behaviour with these small creatures. For example, a child needs to be very calm when handling a rat or they might get nipped, which may result in them dropping and possibly injuring the rat. Once the rat drops to the ground he will most certainly run for the nearest hiding place, and it can then take a while to capture him again. So, very young children are not suitable for rats. A child over eight or nine years old will be a better candidate, since they will have learned a little bit more about animals, and how to treat them.

Can you commit to looking after your rats?

Even if your kids lose interest in the rats, you must be there to clean the cage and feed them. Rats aren't low maintenance – they need attention and care to make sure they live healthy, happy lives. Cages especially can start to smell if left for too long, and a rat is sure to fall ill if he is left more than a week in a dirty cage. So, be prepared for these aspects of rat care. You'll also need to invest in bedding, food, and veterinary treatment whenever it's needed.

What you'll need to keep a rat

Now that the serious questions have been taken care of, it's time to go out and buy all the equipment you need to keep rats. It is much better to make sure you already have all of these items before you bring your rats home. It will make everything easier on the big day. Here are the items you will need:

A suitable home for the rats

The biggest expense involved in buying rats for the first time is, of course, the cage or tank that you're going to keep them in. Don't just buy the first one you come across; spend some time weighing up the pros and cons of each type of housing, for both you and your future pets. For example, some cages are a lot easier to clean out than others. Some cages are much more appealing for rats to live in than others. This is a big decision, so choose wisely.

If your pet shop isn't very well stocked, there are lots of pet supply retailers online that will have a wide variety of cages (some may even have reviews from other rat owners). Here are some tips for making the right choice:

Wire cages provide good ventilation, but they must have a solid floor wire flooring can be very uncomfortable on a rat's paws. The base of the cage must be a few inches deep to prevent the rat from kicking out the bedding all over the floor.

Aquarium or tank style housing has less ventilation, but is generally more escape-proof. However, it will get smelly much quicker because the warm, moist environment creates a breeding ground for bacteria. So these types of housing need to be cleaned out more often than wire cages. They should also never be placed in direct sunlight as they can heat up very quickly. If you choose an aquarium for your rats, it's best to make your own mesh lid for it, which will let in plenty of air.

Some owners also find that making their own housing is a better solution, since it allows them to combine the features of several types of cages into one large home. For example, you could have an aquarium base with a second level on top made from a wire cage. Cages with several levels are a lot more fun for rats.

You absolutely must choose a cage that is a realistic size for several rats. Rats are quite large compared to rodents like mice and hamsters and they need a lot more space. A cage for a chinchilla is probably a better size to choose than one for any other rodent. Rats are very intelligent creatures and will be very bored and unhappy in a cage that is too small or too boring for them.

Accessories for the rats' home

Once you have sourced a suitable home for your rats, you need to fill it with the right accessories and equipment, including:

Food bowl

Get a good ceramic food bowl that your rats can't tip over or chew to pieces. Ceramic is very hygienic and will last a long time too.

Water bottle or water bowl

Water bowls tend to get dirty or get tipped over easily, so they should really only be used if your rats refuse to use a water bottle.

Something to gnaw on

Rats have teeth that grow continuously, and they need to file them down by chewing and gnawing on something hard. There are a few types of rat chews ranging from wooden to stone – it's best to get something from the pet shop that's designed specifically for rats. Many people want to get a tree branch from their gardens, but there are no guarantees that a tree is free from bacteria and insects, so stick with the pet shop where possible. If you do want to use a tree from the garden, wash it thoroughly with soap and water beforehand and put it in the oven for a few minutes to dry it out and kill any bacteria or moulds.

A nesting box

Rats love to curl up in nests where they feel safe and cosy. Choose an enclosed nesting box for your rats with plenty of room for them to turn around in. Fill it with shredded tissue paper or a suitably soft, safe and comfortable bedding.

An exercise wheel

If your cage doesn't come with a wheel, buy one separately. You can get wheels that are stand-alone and don't need to be fixed to bars. Rats do a lot of running in the wild and are still only relatively new to being kept as pets. They need to run for a few hours every night. Make sure the wheel you choose is good quality and won't squeak or rattle in the middle of the night. It should be at least 10 inches in diameter (i.e. significantly bigger than a wheel for a hamster).

Toys

You can put some toys in the tank for your rats to play with, such as cardboard tubes which make great hiding places. If your pet shop has special kiln dried tree branches (this removes all mould and bacteria) then you should get one as your rats will adore having a climbing tree in their tank. Ceramic and wood are much better materials for toys than plastic, which can splinter when chewed and be accidentally ingested. Don't clutter your cage too much with toys though – your rats still need a bit of open space to run about.

A carry case

For trips to the vet, you may want to invest in a small carry case or box. Cardboard shoe boxes can be used, but be warned that rats will easily and quickly chew through the cardboard. So, choose something plastic where possible, or even a small wire cage. Getting a second cage can be very handy if you ever need to separate your rats, for example if one falls ill and needs to be quarantined.

Choosing the right substrate for your rats

The "substrate" is the material you use to fill your rat's tank, in which rats will dig to their heart's content. You need to be very careful about the material you choose for this, as some materials are simply not safe for your little pets.

Here are some tips:
- Shredded cardboard and paper options are usually safe as long as they aren't scented or coloured – newspaper ink should be avoided.
- Avoid cat litter which is unsuitable for rats
- Avoid wood based litter, especially pine and cedar chips which are toxic to rats and cause liver damage
- Make sure you choose bedding and substrates that are free from chemicals, dyes and artificial odours – all bedding must be as natural as possible
- Make sure any nest bedding is safe for your rat to ingest
- Wherever possible, choose bedding materials that have been made specifically for rats, rather than any other pets.

Chapter 4:
Choosing and bringing home your rats

Once you have purchased your checklist of items, the only thing left to do is to choose your rats. This section has some useful advice for choosing healthy rats and making sure you come home with the right pets for you.

Should you buy one rat or several?

Although we have mentioned rat as a singular quite a lot here, you should never buy a single rat as it will be very unhappy living alone. The RSPCA recommends getting same-sex pairs or small groups to start off with. Adult rats that have never met should not be housed with each other and will probably fight.

It is not a good idea to try and introduce new rats to a colony that has already been established the newcomer is likely to be met with aggression. It isn't fair to put the rats through the stress of a stranger, just because you feel like getting another rat. With that in mind, young siblings of the same gender are the best option.

Where to get your rats

Now that you've thought through all of the above, it's safe to say that if you're still reading this, you are serious about getting rats. Congratulations! The fun is only just beginning. Here are some places you can usually get rats from:

Breeders

Before you run off to your local pet shop, do a little bit of research to see if there are any breeders in your area. Rats born and raised in family homes will usually be a lot calmer and tamer than rats who have been raised in the impersonal setting of a pet shop. The babies will have been handled from a young age, and should be friendlier than those that have had no human contact before.

Make sure any breeder you consider can provide you with a reference from someone who has owned one of their rats. They should also be able to tell you all about your chosen rats' family history. If they can't tell you very much, they are probably an amateur breeder and you need to be especially vigilant in making sure their rats are healthy.

Ask to see the babies with the mother if possible, or if they have already been weaned, ask if you can see the mother anyway just to check she is well looked after. In most cases, she will be but it pays to be sure. Since there is little profit to be gained from breeding rats, people usually do it for the love of the animals, so you won't find as many "bad" breeders as you would with, say, puppies for example.

Pet shops

Pet shops need to be approached with caution. You should pay a few visits to a pet shop over time to check on how the rats there are treated. For example, are they left out in draughty places? Are their cages cleaned regularly? Do any of them seem to be ill? Are they provided with enough space to move about in, and an exercise wheel? Do the staff know where the rats came from – were they bred in the pet shop or have they arrived from an outside breeder?

Bear in mind that a rat from a pet shop may not always have had close contact with humans, so you may need to put in some extra work taming it once you get it home.

Also, some of the more unscrupulous pet shops forget to wean their rats at the right time and as a result, you could end up taking home a female that has already fallen pregnant (rats can get pregnant from as young as five weeks old). Be sure to ask about all this before you make a purchase.

Pet shelters

If you're keen to re-home rats that have been abandoned or sur-rendered, then check your local pet shelter to see if they have rats. The advantage of these "pre-loved" rats is that they may already be tamed. You will also be doing a good deed by re-homing a rat colony that really needs a loving family. Rats from pet shelters will have been checked over by a vet to make sure they are healthy enough to be re-homed, which is another advantage for you.

Choosing the right rats from a litter

Now comes the exciting part: choosing the right rats from a litter of pups. Here are some tips:

What to look for...
- rats with bright eyes
- rats that approach you out of curiosity (sometimes a rat will choose you!)
- rats that are active and agile
- rats with a healthy appetite

- rats that move well, with no problems with limping or moving in general

Check that the rats you have your eye on are fully weaned, meaning that they are old enough to eat solid food and be away from the mother.

What to avoid...
- A rat that seems to be scratching a lot on one spot of skin
- A rat that reacts fearfully or aggressively when you put your hand in the cage
- A rat with dull looking or sunken eyes
- rats with runny faeces or faeces hanging from their fur
- rats with signs of discharge coming from the nose, eyes or rear end, or signs of sneezing, wheezing or coughing

Check that the rats, if old enough to reproduce, have not been living with rats of the opposite sex and are not pregnant as a result

Choosing a pair or group of rats

It goes without saying at this stage that your rats will need to be of the same gender if they're going to live happily together (without making lots of baby rats!). If they come from the same litter, this is even better, and will mean no fisticuffs when they reach maturity. If you are planning to introduce rats that aren't siblings, it must be while they are still young – between 5 and 9 weeks old is the safest time for introductions.

Should you get males or females?

It is entirely up to you whether you choose to keep male rats or female rats. However, lots of people say that males are slightly calmer and more docile, and are also a bit larger making them easier to handle. Males will play fight occasionally, but if they are siblings that have always been together they will not fight properly and should get on fine.

Females, on the other hand, are said to be a bit more active and curious than their male counterparts, and will want to explore their surroundings rather than sit still. Females will come into heat every 4 to 5 days, and you may notice some slight changes in posture, as well as some ear wagging during those times. Despite these differences, all rats are individuals with their own unique personalities, so it's important not to make too many generalisations.

Transporting your rats

Your little rats are probably going to be stressed when making the journey from where they were raised to your home. To make things easier, you need to transport them in a safe, comfortable container.

It should have:
- Air holes for breathing
- A durable material, preferably not cardboard which can easily get soiled or chewed during the journey
- Some soft, cosy bedding to make the journey comfortable

Ideally, some bedding that was originally in your rats' old enclosure, so that they have something that smells familiar around them for the first couple of days (you can take this and put it in the new nesting box when you get home).

Arriving home with your rats

Ask your pet shop or breeder to provide you with some of the same food your chosen rats have been eating all along, so that you don't have to abruptly switch their diet to something new on top of all the other new changes in their environment.

Once you get home, place the container inside the tank and let your rats to walk out of it into the cage by themselves, if you can. This will minimise an already stressful situation by not forcing them to be handled just yet.

Before you do anything else, make sure your rats' housing is in a suitable area of the house.

That means somewhere that:
- Is away from draughts and direct sunlight
- Is inaccessible to other pets, whose smells can be very stressful to rats
- Is peaceful during the day time so that the rats can enjoy their naps
- Has plenty of activity in the evenings so your rats can be where your family spends the most time (the lounge is ideal)
- Won't wake anyone up at night, when the rats might be running on the wheel

Chapter 5:
Taming and handling your rats

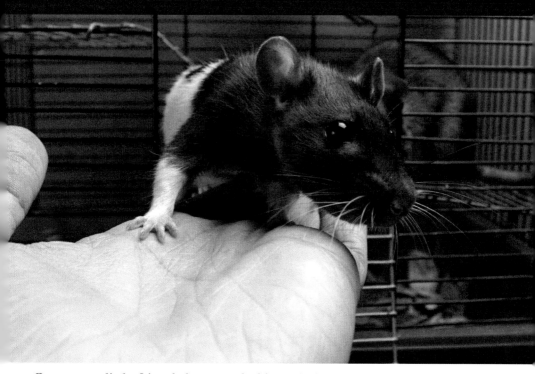

Once your little friends have settled into their new home environment, you can start the process of getting them used to being handled. Some people may be lucky enough to get rats that have already been socialised (meaning they are already used to people). If this is the case, you'll just need to get each rat used to your smell. Usually though, a new baby rat will need at least a little bit of careful taming before he gets really used to being handled. This section will help you to do that.

Taming and handling individuals

Handling is one of the few activities that need to be done on each individual rat. Trying to do this for all rats at once will only lead to trouble. So, take each stage slowly and make sure you can tell your rats apart, otherwise you will end up with one tame rat and one timid one. Spend at least 20 minutes each day handling each rat, for the first week or so.

Being persistent

Before you begin trying to handle a new rat, make sure your expectations are realistic. Some rats take longer to become tame than others. Don't let that put you off. A very small number of frustrated rat owners simply give up and simply leave their rats in the cage to live out a wild existence. This is a really bad idea, as it makes it really stressful for your rat whenever he has to be handled – for example, if you bring him to the vet, or even if you need to move him to a container while you clean his cage. It is very sad to see a rat that never gets handled. So, make sure you keep going with the handling until your rat is calm enough to climb onto your hands voluntarily. It will be worth it!

Staying calm

Above all, you need to stay calm when handling your rat for the first time. One thing you could do if you're nervous is have a friend that has already tamed a rat to visit and help with the process. Really though, your rat needs to get used to being handled by you first and foremost, and adding too many people into the mix is going to be overwhelming for him. Your rat needs to have positive experiences of being handled from the very start, or he will grow to associate your hands with a bad situation. So, make sure you're in a calm, positive frame of mind before you begin. Having a "can do" attitude is important.

How to handle nipping

If you have a particularly nippy little rat, you could wear gloves at the beginning if it makes you feel calmer. Once the rat gets used to the idea of being held and walking on your hands, you can phase out the gloves. When you feel calmer, your rat will feel calmer, and the nipping will stop.

Try some treats

If you want your rat to feel distracted and to associate handling with something rewarding, you can use treats at the very beginning. Some particularly tempting fruit or vegetables cut into tiny pieces should do the trick. Treats do a great job of distracting a nervous rat and making sure he enjoys the moment.

Choose somewhere with a soft landing

Before you take your rat out and handle him, you need to choose somewhere safe to do so. That means somewhere with a very soft landing, like the couch or the bed. If you stand up when handling your rat for the first time you are probably going to find he jumps out of your hands, or you get nipped and you drop him. You don't want him to have a huge fall when this happens. So, either sit on the carpet with your rat's cage just in front of you or choose a large couch to put the cage on and sit beside it. It's also a good idea to choose a room that is secure, with all windows and doors closed and no nooks and crannies for an escaped rat to hide away in. Make sure no one is going to walk into the room and interrupt you either – that could give you or your rat a fright, or if your rat is on the loose it could lead to him getting out of the room.

Step by step guide to handing

Here is a step-by-step guide to the very first time you try to handle your rat. Good luck! It's a good idea to wear old clothes at first, and put some newspaper down, as timid rats can relieve themselves on you out of nervousness. In general, rats will also scent mark with urine, so have some tissues ready in case.

1. Begin by getting your rat used to your smell. If you can put your hand inside the cage slowly without him flinching or hiding away, you are making progress. So, try to get to that stage before anything else. He should grow used to the idea that those giant hands of yours are nothing to be feared, and that they often bring gifts in the shape of delicious treats. Try spending an evening near the cage, speaking to the rats softly and putting your hand in at hourly intervals.

2. Get your rat to the stage where he is brave enough to approach your hands. This might take you a few minutes, or it might take a day or two. It depends on the rat. Usually the best way to do this is to hold a small treat in the palm of your hand (inside the cage) and wait for curiosity to get the better of him. He will soon be at the stage where he crawls onto the palm of your hand to get the treat. Stay calm and still when he does. Repeat this several times over a few hours so he gets the idea.

3. Once you're sure your rat is comfortable venturing onto your hand, you can progress to slowly moving your hand out of the cage when he is on it. If he's a bigger rat, you will probably need two hands to make a little platform for him. This is much less stressful for him than being grabbed out of the blue. When you make a grab for a rat it seems like an attack from a predator, so try to avoid this practice wherever pos-sible. Instead, you should let your rat make his way onto your hand in his own time, at least until he is properly tamed. If he is really curious he might decide to exit the cage by himself, by running up your arm. Remember that we are trying to create only positive, rewarding expe-riences for your rat so that he gets more and more comfortable with being handled. Your rat might panic at this stage and jump off your hand back into the cage. If he does, don't worry. Just try again later.

4. When you can successfully move your hand (or hands) out of the cage with your rat on them, you can then start to properly handle him. If both parties are calm, this should go well. A lot of rats like to explore their immediate surroundings, so don't expect yours to sit per-fectly still on your lap. One technique you could use at the beginning is to have a soft hat to put the rat in which will feel like a nest and make your rat feel a little bit calmer.

5. Now it's time to get your rat used to being picked up, rather than simply using your hands as an elevator every time. To do this, put him in an enclosure with an open top but that he can't climb out of, like the bath or a box with very high sides. That way, you'll be able to practice picking him up rather than having to tempt him out of

the awkwardly shaped cage every time. Put a few distractions in the enclosure, like food and bedding, so he doesn't feel distressed. Then, simply use your two hands to lift the rat – ideally, one hand should go under the tummy and one should support the rear end. You are now going to scoop up your rat with your two hands, gently – not too quickly, or he will get a fright, but not so slowly that he has the chance to climb out of your hands before you've moved them off the ground.

6. You want to use the most gentle, unobtrusive way of picking up your rat, which is usually just a simple scooping method. Some people use more severe methods like pinching the scruff of the neck – these aren't necessary, and they aren't very nice for a fragile little rat to experience. NEVER pick up a rat by the tail. Rats aren't toys and they shouldn't be handled roughly or carelessly – they are fragile creatures that need respect from their owners. Once you've spent thirty minutes to an hour practising this scooping method, the rat should be at ease with it. There should never be any need to use a different method, unless your rat is having his teeth clipped or being examined by a vet.

A word about children and rats

If you have young children, please don't give them the responsibility of taming their own rat, especially if they haven't had a pet before. Children can be rough, and often get over-excited, forgetting that they are playing with a very real living thing that has delicate internal organs and can get frightened easily. Please tame each rat yourself before teaching your children how to handle it properly, and even then, please supervise your child until they are old enough to be trusted.

How to capture an escaped rat

It is an inevitable fact that someday, somehow, your rat is going to escape its cage or escape your grasp and run free somewhere in your house. When that happens, there are a few important things to do.

Alert everyone in the house that there is a rat on the loose. Everyone needs to remove their shoes, and watch out where they are stepping and sitting.

Close all the windows and all the doors in the house. Each room should be sealed off to contain the rat, even if you're not sure which room he is in. Lock away any other pets immediately.

Now go to the room where you suspect your rat could be (if you don't know, simply follow these steps for each room one by one).

Spend a few minutes in the room sitting absolutely still and listening very carefully. When a rat is on the loose you can usually hear it – eating carpet is a favourite activity, and even just running on the floorboards with its little feet can be heard. You might be lucky enough to catch a glimpse of him if you are vigilant enough.

Leave a particularly pungent smelling treat out in the centre of the room and sit nearby. Rats have an excellent sense of smell and it shouldn't be too long before yours comes running to see what tasty treat is there.

Once he's out in the open, you can drop a tea towel over him, a bucket or even a box. Then you can reach under it and pick him up. You can also try a long tube if you have one – rats love dark little hiding holes. Simply wait till he's entered the tube and then block the ends.

If those methods fail, try setting up a humane trap and checking the trap first thing in the morning. Some escapees can take days or even weeks to be coaxed back into captivity, so don't give up! If your rat is tame though, curiosity will get the better of him and you shouldn't have a huge problem.

Chapter 6:
Feeding your rats

Congratulations! You have come this far and you're now ready to start a daily care routine for your new little friends. This chapter will go through the kind of diet your rats need in order to keep them happy and healthy.

Feeding your rats

Twice a day your little pet needs to be fed with pellet food that's been made specifically for rats, which you can buy from the pet shop. The RSPCA recommends feeding your rats once in the morning and once at night. Make sure the food you buy is good quality, with plenty of different nutrients included.

Note: you should never feed your rats cereal or muesli that has been made for human consumption; this will be far too sugary and filled with ingredients your rats do not need. Stick to foods that have been produced specifically for rats.

At the same time, you should also avoid foods that have been made for animals like rabbits, guinea pigs and hamsters. Rats have specific dietary needs that these foods won't address, and there are lots of amino acids, vitamins and minerals that their bodies can't make by themselves.

Giving treats

In addition to the staple rat food diet, you can also add some treats to your rats' menu. It's very easy to find things in your fridge that a rat will eat (fruits, nuts and vegetables are always good ideas) so there should be no need to buy any of the processed, packaged treats you'll see in pet shops.

Treats should be given sparingly; you don't want to upset your rats' tummies by giving them too much fruit and veg in one go. Don't pile up the food bowl with treats, just give a few small pieces. It's a good idea to scatter treats around your rat's cage (avoiding the corners he uses as toilet areas) in order to mimic the foraging they would naturally do in the wild.

Here are some treats your rats will probably love:
- Cucumber
- Carrot
- Apple
- Broccoli
- Pear
- Celery
- Blackberries
- Blueberries
- Chicory
- Alfalfa
- Courgette
- Mange tout

- Green beans
- Cress
- Spinach
- Sweetcorn
- Turnip

Make sure all of the above treats are cut into tiny pieces that will be easy for your rats to eat. Also, wash everything thoroughly beforehand. Today's fruit and veg is treated with a lot of chemicals which could harm a rat.

Protein for rats

Rats are omnivores and in the wild they would eat insects. Whilst we don't suggest you feed them insects, you can give your rats protein in the form of low fat cottage cheese or cooked pieces of egg. Nuts are also a great source of protein, but rats can get ill if they are given too many fatty foods, so always feed these treats in moderation.

Foods that rats can't eat

Make sure everyone in your family knows that they can't feed your rats the following foods, as they are likely to make them quite sick:
- Blue cheese – the mould is toxic to rats
- Raisins and grapes
- Licorice – poisonous and causes neurological damage
- Green bananas – very bad for the digestion of starch
- Onion
- Avocado skin and stone – toxic, but the avocado itself is fine
- Raw artichokes – inhibit the digestion of protein
- Raw red cabbage and brussel sprouts
- Raw sweet potato – produces cyanides in the stomach
- Raw meat and raw tofu – contain too much bacteria
- Raw kidney beans
- Raw potato and raw potato tops
- Tomato leaves
- Rhubarb and rhubarb leaves – contain toxic oxalates

- Walnut
- Citrus fruits, especially mango and orange juice, which cause cancer in male rats
- Human foods, especially chocolate
- Insects from your garden – may carry harmful parasites

Food safety

Don't guess what your rats might be able to eat. Always check with your vet if you aren't sure.

Old food

Every day, you should do a quick scan of your rats' cage and nesting box and remove any food that is stale or has been there for too long. This will make sure your rats don't eat anything that makes them ill, and it will also make their home a more hygienic place to live.

Water

Rats in captivity needs access to fresh water at all times. You should change the water in their bottle or bowl every day, even if you think it looks clean. Water that is left stagnant can go stale, and might also be a breeding ground for algae which is a green slimey substance that may harm your pets.

Supplements

There should be no need to give your rats vitamin supplements as long as you are feeding them a balanced, varied diet of rat pellets and fresh foods. The only time you might need to give extra vitamin and mineral supplements is if your rats fall ill and your vet has advised you to. Giving large amounts of supplements can throw a rat's system out of balance and may even make them feel worse. So, only give these under the direction of your vet.

Chapter 7:
A guide to rat health

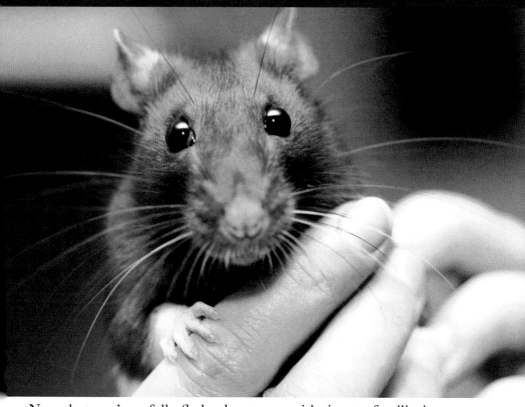

Now that you're a fully-fledged rat owner, it's time to familiarise yourself with rat health in general. It's important to know the signs of illness in your little pets and also to know what is and isn't healthy – it could save you a trip to the vet someday. This chapter will give you the facts you need to know.

Your responsibility

Since rats are hardy little creatures, a lot of the problems that arise are due to improper care on the part of their owners. To prevent yourself from being to blame for your rats falling ill, you need to:

- Feed a healthy, balanced diet with no surprise ingredients, no processed foods and no substances that are toxic to rats
- Clean your rat's cage once a week at the very least, thoroughly washing and disinfecting the housing and toys each time.
- Keep the cage in a warm, dry room in a position that is out of direct sunlight
- Use only rat friendly bedding and substrates in the tank
- Don't subject your rats to stressful situations like being around other pets, having strange rats introduced to their colony, being handled roughly or being made to put up with chemicals in their environment such as cigarette smoke, aerosol spray, or incense.

Those are just some of the precautions you can take to make sure your rats stay healthy. Another important measure is to take them to the vet as soon as you see anything unusual in their appearance or behaviour. What's more, if you suspect something infectious, all rats in the colony will need to be seen by a vet and not just the rat with the symptoms.

Knowing the signs of illness

A good rat owner knows the classic signs of illness, and is always vigilant for any of the following signs that something is wrong:
- Loss of appetite – food is left unfinished or untouched
- Lethargy and listlessness when the rat is normally active and alert
- Rat stays in the nesting box at times when it would usually be out and about
- Dull or sunken eyes
- Diarrhoea, or sticky, wet faeces which sometimes get matted in the fur
- Discharge or redness coming from the nose, eyes or rear end
- Sneezing, coughing or wheezing
- A hard, swollen tummy
- Signs of injury, such as trailing a limb or limping
- Difficulty walking or seeming off-balance
- Scratching a lot on the same area of skin
- Abnormal bumps or lumps on the body, cuts or sores

- Behavioural changes, such as suddenly not wanting to be handled, being unusually aggressive, or simply sleeping around the clock instead of waking up to exercise

Knowing when to visit the vet

The list above should be very helpful in deciding whether to take your rats to the vet. If you spot any of the above symptoms, you should book a vet's appointment as soon as you can. In particular, if you have children who normally handle your rat, you should teach them about the signs above and what to look for. Once a week, you should look over the rats yourself just to make sure they are healthy.

Common rat diseases

Here are some of the more well-known rat diseases and injuries that experienced owners come across:

Bald patches and fur loss

If your rat suddenly seems to have patches of fur missing, there could be a problem. Firstly, it could be that your rat has mites, which are a tiny parasite that cause itching and a lot of stress. Your rat will rub his body against the sides of the cage and will be persistently scratching and biting at the affected areas, causing the fur to fall out.

Mites need to be treated by a vet as they cause your rat a lot of discomfort and are also contagious between pets. So, the bedding and cage of a rat with mites will need to be cleaned and disinfected thoroughly to kill all the mites. You will need to do this very regularly whilst your rat is being treated. Topical sprays are normally used, and if you have a group of rats the whole colony will need to be treated.

Mange is a condition caused by mites, usually in the rat's ears. They can cause an allergic reaction in your rat leading to scabs and sores on the fur – a very sore and uncomfortable condition for your little pet. Creams, oral medications and injections can be used to kill off the mange, and any sores can be soothed with topical treatments.

Other causes of fur loss can be malnutrition, stress or fighting between rats. Your vet should be able to make a proper diagnosis on examining your rat.

Mycoplasma

Most rats are carriers of a disease called Mycoplasma which causes respiratory problems, but cannot affect humans. It's thought that rats catch the disease from their mothers as they travel through the birth canal – rats born by caesarean don't usually have the illness. Since rats are carriers, they may not show any symptoms until they have flare-ups at certain points in their lives.

Symptoms include wheezing, sneezing and breathing difficulties. Wet noses are also a common symptom, as well as Porphyrin, which is a red coloured discharge from the eyes and nose. Look out for reddish brown stains around the cage where they have sneezed, and on lighter coloured rats you might see these rusty stains on the fur. The symptoms can be treated with medication, but there is no cure and the rat will always be a carrier of Mycoplasma.

Rats with good immune systems will live long lives despite having the disease. Adding vitamin A and E to the diet of rats suffering from Mycoplasma can make a difference to their recovery. Visiting the vet is a good idea, to rule out other respiratory issues like pneumonia.

Porphyrin

Special glands in a rat's eyes produce a light red discharge called Porphyrin. Don't be alarmed if you see this around the eyes and nose of your rat – it isn't blood, and is a natural bodily fluid. If there is too much of this discharge being produced then your rat may be stressed or under the weather. If this is the case your rat needs to pay a visit to your vet for a check-up.

Poisoning

If one of your rats has come into contact with anything toxic, or he has accidentally eaten something harmful, he needs to go to the vet.

Some substances which are toxic to rats include:
- Rodent poison
- Flea powder
- Pesticides on fruit and vegetables
- Household cleaning chemicals
- Foxglove plants
- Chocolate
- Ivy
- Rhubarb and rhubarb leaves
- Oleander

Signs of poisoning include a shivering rat, or one that is losing consciousness. If your rat suddenly loses consciousness it could also be from carbon monoxide in the air. If you suspect this is the case you need to call in some experts to have your home checked.

Detached tail and de-gloving

One very unique feature of the rat's biology is that it can actually shed part of its tail when it is frightened. The tail can actually lose the top layer of skin at the very end, known as de-gloving. This leaves a very pink, new layer of skin and muscle exposed at the very tip of the tail, which will eventually dry out and fall off. If it doesn't do this naturally and it seems sore and inflamed, you may need your vet to take a look at it. As soon as de-gloving happens you should treat the tail with a pet friendly antiseptic to prevent infection.

Ear infections and cysts

If a rat seems to have a permanent head tilt, it could be the result of an inner ear infection which has an effect on the rat's balance. Rats with this issue often walk in circles and seem off balance. Sometimes this condition is treatable with antibiotics and the rat will recover.

However, if the problem is caused by a cyst then it is usually untreatable (though the rat will have a perfectly normal life besides having balance issues).

Strep infections

Strep throat in humans (an infection causing a sore throat) can be passed to rats and can be fatal within three days or so. If you have a sore throat, do not handle your rat until you feel better.

Bumblefoot

Bumblefoot is an infection in the rat's foot which causes it to get very sore and red and swell up. It looks like a rounded, red swelling and can form a yellowish crust. There is no cure for this, but you can prevent it with a few careful steps. For one thing, you should always have a solid flooring on your cage as opposed to a wire mesh flooring which can irritate the sensitive balls of the feet. Secondly, keep the cage very clean to avoid infections in the feet. Thirdly, any rats that are gaining weight should be put on low calorie diets to trim down, as excess weight on the feet can turn into Bumblefoot.

Eye issues

Rats are very prone to eye issues including irritations, infections and cataracts. Each time you handle your rat you should look closely at the eyes to make sure they are bright, clear and healthy. Many rats with eye problems that go unnoticed end up losing their eyes.

Chapter 8

Rat FAQs

This chapter will deal with some of your most commonly asked questions on keeping rats. You can keep this book and refer to it throughout your career as a rat enthusiast. It may come in very handy.

How often should I clean out my rat's cage? And how should I do it?

You should do a full clean of your rats' cage at least once a week. Never leave it to the stage where it gets smelly, or where there are faeces everywhere. Your little rats rely on you to keep their home clean and they will be very unhappy and unhealthy if left somewhere dirty. Some tips for cleaning out your rats' cage include:

Find somewhere safe to put your rats while you're cleaning the cage. Bathtubs are often a good idea because your rats can't climb out of them.

Start by emptying all of the substrate out of the base of the cage into a bin bag. Then, empty out all of the bedding and old food from the nesting box.

Disinfect the walls and base of the tank, the wheel and the food bowl, as well as the nesting box. Some cleaning solution in a bucket of hot water and a few wet cloths should do the trick. Clean the base until no trace of dirt or debris remains.

Rinse everything you have just washed in fresh water, so that there is no trace of disinfectant left behind (it contains harmful chemicals which could affect your rats).

Dry everything thoroughly. Then, put down a fresh layer of paper in the bottom of the tank, and cover it with several inches of substrate for burrowing. Put new bedding into the clean, dry nesting box and replace the clean food bowl with fresh food. Once the cage is back together, your rats can be put back into their lovely clean home.

How do I tell if a rat is male or female?

In adult rats, a female has noticeable nipples on the underside of her tummy. In younger rats, simply hold the tail up and look at the rat's rear end. Female rats have two little holes (one for pee and babies and one for poo) which are quite close together, whereas in males the holes are noticeably further apart.

Can I give my rats a bath? How else can I keep them clean?

If your rat has something dirty matted in his fur, you can use a tooth-brush to get it out, or you can simply clip away the soiled fur. If, how-ever, the rat is beginning to smell then you can give it the occasional bath. Use a very mild shampoo designed for small animals, and rinse very, very thoroughly. Afterwards, towel dry the rat and keep him somewhere warm until he dries off completely. Don't shampoo too often because it removes the natural oils from the fur and makes it too dry and dull.

Can I toilet train my rat?

Believe it or not, some owners manage to successfully train their rats to pee in a particular spot in their cages. A little tray of substrate is a good thing to try, or even just a shallow little box in the corner of the cage, so that the rest of the cage stays clean and dry. Fill the toilet tray with some sawdust that has already been peed on and a couple of faeces. With a bit of luck, your rat will soon get the idea that this is where the toilet is.

Rats are very clean animals and usually go to the toilet in one corner of the cage anyway. This way, you can actually remove the soiled tray and replace it throughout the week, so that there is no smell in the cage between the weekly clean out.

I've heard rats can be trained to do tricks. Is this true?

Yes, many rat owners manage to teach their rats tricks like coming when they are called, begging for food and staying put. This is done with a technique called positive reinforcement, where the rat is rewarded with a treat when it behaves in the right way. Rats are very intelligent and most respond well to this type of training.

Can I let my rat run around the house?

You can let your rat run free as long as it's in a safe, secured room with the doors and windows closed. All potential hazards should be out of the way, for example cables which could be chewed, or unfamiliar house plants which your rat might try to eat. Don't attempt to let your rat run free until he is fully tamed or you will have a real problem catching him again. Bear in mind that once your rat gets a taste for freedom he will want to be out running around all of the time!

Conclusion

We hope you've enjoyed this book and that you have learned enough about rats to be a responsible, conscientious rat owner. Becoming the owner of one of these charismatic creatures is a very rewarding experience, and you are going to have a lot of fun in the days and months to come. You'll see for yourself how these cheeky and funny little pets managed to charm their way out of laboratories and into people's homes and families. May you and your rats have many happy times together!

Want to know more about looking after your pet?

The writer of this book, Dr. Gordon Roberts, is a veterinarian and owns a total of eight animal hospitals around the UK. He believes that the key to a healthy, happy pet is preventative care, which is only possible when pet owners take the initiative to educate themselves about their animals. As a result, Gordon has written dozens of useful reports on pet care in order to share his years of experience with discerning pet owners. As a thank you for purchasing this book, you can browse and download his specialist reports completely free of charge! You'll learn all sorts of useful information about how to spot possible health conditions early on, and how to make preventative care for your pet a priority, helping you save time and money on visits to the vet later on. To view and download these bonus reports, simply visit Gordon's website at: http://drgordonroberts.com/freereportsdownload/.

Best wishes,
Gordon

Made in the USA
Middletown, DE
16 June 2025